Noah and t...

Illustrated by Ron Kauffman

Written By: **Kim Mitzo Thompson, Karen Mitzo Hilderbrand, Ken Carder**
Executive Producers: **Kim Mitzo Thompson, Karen Mitzo Hilderbrand**
Book Design: **Jennifer Birchler**

Twin Sisters Productions
4710 Hudson Drive
Stow, OH 44224 USA
www.twinsisters.com   1-800-248-8946

ISBN-13: 978-159922-438-1

"Noah, you are a good man," said God. "But from heaven I see how wicked and evil most people have become. It makes me sad. So, Noah, I'm going to put an end to all people and destroy the earth." Noah listened very carefully as God spoke to him. "But Noah, I promise you and your family will be safe."

"Noah, I want you to build an ark out of cypress wood. Make the ark 450 feet long, 75 feet wide, and 45 feet high. Make a roof on top. Put a door in the side. Inside the ark, build lower, middle, and upper decks, each with a lot of rooms," said God. Noah listened, making certain he understood God's instructions.

"You are to bring into the ark two of all living creatures, male and female, to keep them alive with you. Two of every kind of bird, of every kind of animal and of every kind of creature that moves along the ground will come to you. You are also to take enough food for you and for the animals," said God.

Noah and his sons, Shem, Ham and Japheth, together with his wife and the wives of his three sons, entered the ark. They had with them every wild animal, all livestock according to their kinds, every creature that moves along the ground and every bird. Noah did everything just as God commanded him. Noah was 600 years old.

Soon the rain began to fall. The rain continued forty days and forty nights. The ark floated on the surface of the water as the waters soon covered all the high mountains on the earth. The waters flooded the earth for 150 days. Only Noah and those with him in the ark survived.

The waters slowly went down and the ark came to rest on the mountain of Ararat. Noah opened a window in the ark. He sent out a dove to see if the water had completely gone away and if there was dry ground. The dove returned in the evening with a freshly plucked olive leaf in its beak. Noah knew the water was gone.

Finally, God said to Noah, "Come out of the ark, you and your wife and your family. Bring out the animals and all the creatures so they can multiply on the earth and increase in number."

So Noah and his family and the animals and creatures came out. Noah built an altar to the Lord and worshipped. God saw Noah's worship and said, "Never again will I destroy all living creatures as I have done." Noah listened carefully.

"Noah, this is a sign of my promise to you and to all the earth," added God. Suddenly the most brilliant rainbow appeared in the sky stretching as far as the eye could see. "I will remember my promise," said God. Noah, his family, and the animals were happy.

Draw your favorite animals leaving the ark.